The
ASSAULT
on LIBERTY

Rambling Thoughts
of a Roads Scholar

The
ASSAULT
on LIBERTY

Rambling Thoughts
of a Roads Scholar

By Mason McCoy

LANGDON STREET PRESS

MINNEAPOLIS, MN

Langdon Street Press
212 3rd Avenue North, Suite 290
Minneapolis, MN 55401
612.455.2293
www.langdonstreetpress.com

ISBN - 978-1-936183-07-4
ISBN - 1-936183-07-2
LCCN - 2010924840

Cover Design by Alan Pranke
Typeset by James Arneson

Printed in the United States of America

(ACKNOWLEDGMENT)

I dedicate this book to my wife Sally. She was always there as a sounding board to bounce ideas off and to make suggestions. It was her belief in me and what I was doing that kept me going. Without her loving patience whenever I was staring into space pondering how to word the next paragraph and ignoring the "honey dos", this book would have died in its early stages.

INTRODUCTION

I am not your typical author; I didn't graduate from some Ivy League university. I am not even one of the talking heads you see on TV. In fact, I am not an author at all. If Miss Walker, my high school English teacher is still with us (she would have to be close to 100), I am afraid that the shock of my writing this book will send her to her grave.

In a lot of ways I am like "Joe the Plumber" we got to know during the 2008 election. I am just the guy down the street in Anytown, U.S.A. that drove a truck all his life. Forty-five years and nearly four million miles of driving has afforded me a lot of time to think things through. That's how you become a "Roads Scholar."

I love my God, I love my family, and I love my country. I have been married to the love of my life for forty-five years; we raised three sons and have six grandchildren. I love them all very dearly, and I am scared to death that they will not be living in the "One nation under God, indivisible, with liberty and justice for all."

I think most people feel the same frustration that I feel. We can see the crash coming, but no one hears our screams, no one seems to care! I can call my Congressman, but he is a Republican in a Democratic controlled Congress and is a voice in the wilderness, just like I am. I can call my Senators, but they are Dianne Feinstein and Barbara Boxer; I might as well call Loony Tunes and talk to Daffy Duck.

This book is my scream of frustration. It is my attempt to reach other people who love this great nation as I do, and hopefully I can be a spark to help light a fire of patriotism and unity to bring us together again as one nation under God.

All societies must be governed by some force; ultimately there are only two forces that govern men. Mankind must be controlled either by a power within themselves or be controlled by an external power. The power within relies on personal moral restraint which comes from God. With it come the inalienable rights of life, liberty, and the pursuit of happiness. The less we rely on the internal power and self-government, the more we are controlled by the external power, which is public law or physical force, and, at the extreme, the iron fist of tyranny. It is my goal to show that by throwing God under the bus, we are also throwing our liberty and freedom under the bus.

CHAPTER
ONE

ARE WE A CHRISTIAN NATION?

I live in Northern California; I don't mean Sacramento or the San Francisco Bay area that most people from Southern California refer to as Northern California. I mean the Northern California that is two hundred and fifty miles north of Sacramento, next to the Oregon State line. We can get some pretty severe winter weather here, which we have had the last few weeks. This morning dawned with a beautiful clear blue sky, the air was crystal clear, and you could see forever. I poured a cup of coffee and sat on our front deck to absorb some of the beauty.

Mt. Shasta, in all of its majestic beauty, sits right at the end of our driveway. Even though it is thirty miles away, it looks like you could reach out and touch it. It has a fresh covering of snow from the recent storms contrasted by the blue sky. It is a breathtaking sight that could only have been painted by the hand of God.

We have lived here for close to thirty years and the mountain, as beautiful as it is, has become almost invisible. With the exception of a few moments like this morning, when its beauty shouts so loud you can't ignore it, I hardly ever look up and take in its beauty. I remember when we first moved into this house, I couldn't walk out the front door or pass the front window without pausing for a second to gaze at the mountain. Over time we get accustomed to an object of beauty, we take it for granted, and it is "just there".

I think we have a tendency to do the same thing with our liberty; it is a thing of breathtaking beauty that is "just there". Few Americans know what it is to be without liberty, and few give any thought of the price our forefathers paid for it. Liberty to most Americans is sort of like air or sex, not all that important until they aren't getting any!

Unlike Mt. Shasta, which will be there regardless, liberty takes a lot of maintenance to prevent it from crumbling away and, sad to say, we have been neglecting it.

I have reached the point in my life where those old geezers in their 70's don't look nearly as old as they used to, and I can see the changes that have taken place in our society and government over the years that the younger generations haven't seen. There have been many changes in my lifetime, some positive, some negative. On the positive side the technological changes have been mind boggling, from the mechanical adding machine of my youth to the computers of today. I remember when I was six years old I got blood poisoning. I had a red stripe up my arm and I had to sit for what, to a six year old, seemed like weeks with my arm in a tub of epsom salts solution to get rid of the infection because antibiotics were not available yet.

In 1949 my father died of a heart attack at the age of 42. If the medical technology of today had been available then, he would have had an excellent chance for recovery. There is seemingly no end to the positive changes I could write about, but this book is going to be about the negative changes, the erosion of our nation's morality and the threats to our liberty.

With my field of expertise being in truck driving, instead of writing, it is my hope and prayer that I am able to convey my thoughts on where our nation is headed and the real dangers I see for our liberty and freedom. If you're thinking here's another one of those Republican right wing radicals, I admit it, but my thoughts on our liberty and freedom are non-partisan. I think the Democratic Party is a few paces ahead, leading the way down the road of self destruction, but the Republican Party is hot in its tracks.

I have had the feeling that something was not right with our government my whole adult life. Like most people not being able to put my finger on the problem, I just went to work every day with my head down and my rear up, not paying much attention to what was going on in government. I just tried to get to the end of the month before the end of the paycheck; the only time I paid attention was at election time. I have always had the opinion that if someone didn't vote, he didn't have the right to gripe, and I usually had something to gripe about.

The first year I was old enough to vote was 1964, the Lyndon Johnson and Barry Goldwater election. Ronald Reagan was campaigning for Goldwater, and I was very impressed with Ronald Reagan's G.E. speeches and his "Time to Choose" speech at the Republican Convention; he was saying what I wanted to hear. I have always wanted the government to do fewer favors for me and keep its hand out of my pocket. Over the years I started to notice that it didn't make any difference whether the Republicans or Democrats were in office. We still ended up with bigger government, more taxes, more regulations, more deficit spending, less liberty, and more politicians out of touch with their constituents.

The Constitution limits the Federal Government's duties to the tasks the individual states cannot do for the collective good of the nation, such as providing national security, regulating commerce, and securing our borders. If electing conservative Republicans isn't going to hold the government to the constitution, what is it going to take? What are we missing?

Are we the one nation under God that all the plaques on national monuments and government buildings say we are? Do we trust in God like it says on our currency? No doubt the faith of our Founding Fathers has suffered some erosion over time, but I cannot be convinced that we have slipped to the point that President Obama says we have; that we are no longer a Christian nation.

There has been a movement to remove God from our government and society since the very start of our nation. Early on, there was a very strong Christian resistance to counter any attempt of excluding God. Its first big toe-hold was in the late 1830s when public schools came into being. Before that all schools were Christian schools, and there was a time that one of the school books was the Holy Bible. They weren't called Christian Schools; it was a no-brainer—Christianity was part of the school curriculum. There has been a subtle and unrelenting pressure over the years to undermine the Christian principles. During the last forty years, this pressure has been about as subtle as a sledge hammer and has been very successful. For all practical purposes God has been expelled from school!

With the removal of God from our schools, there has been a growing doubt and ignorance of our Christian heritage. Some deny that our laws are based on God's laws, or that the Founding Fathers were Christian. James Madison said to the Virginia General Assembly in 1778:

> *"We have staked the whole future of American civilization, not on the power of government, far from it. We've staked the future of all our political institutions upon our capacity...to sustain ourselves according to the Ten Commandments of God."*

The Christian influence of the Ten Commandments on our laws is pretty obvious. In many other areas it is not quite so obvious. In the book of Joshua when the Israelites reached the Promised Land, compare the similarities of how the land was divided up amongst the people and how the settlers of the American West were given land grants by the Homestead Act of 1862. This simple act of providing land ownership secured liberty, industry, and patriotism. James Madison developed the concept of checks and balances with the three branches of government, the Judicial, Legislative, and Executive. Where did the inspiration for that come from?

Isaiah 33:22 *"For the Lord is our judge, The Lord is our lawgiver, The Lord is our King; It is He who will save us."*

John McLean, Supreme Court Justice from 1830 to 1861, on the relationship of Christianity and Civil Government said:

"For many years my hope for the perpetuity of our institutions has rested upon Bible morality and the general dissemination of Christian principles. This is an element which did not exist in the ancient republics. It is a basis on which free governments may be maintained through all time.

"It is a truth experienced in all time that a free government can have no other than a moral basis; and it requires a high degree of intelligence and virtue in the people to maintain it. Free government is not a self-moving machine. It can only act through agencies. And if its aims be low and selfish, if it addresses itself to the morbid feelings of humanity, its tendencies must be corrupt and weaken the great principles on which it is founded.

"Our mission of freedom is not carried out by brute force, by canon law, or any other law except the moral law and those Christian principles which are found in the Scriptures."

We can read in the book of Exodus where God led His people out of Egypt through the desert to the Promised Land. How many of us can grasp the latter day version where God led His people from the Old World to the New World and to the Promised Land? Our Founding Fathers understood that they had been led to the Promised Land by God, just as the Israelites had been led to the Promised Land.

Thomas Jefferson, for one, alluded to it in his second inaugural address. Thomas Jefferson is the one whose Christianity seems to be attacked the most; it appears to be general knowledge that he was an atheist. To quote him from his second inaugural address as President of the United States:

"I shall need the favor of that Being in whose hands we are, who led our fathers, as Israel of old, from their native land, and planted them in a country flowing with all the necessaries and comforts of life; who has covered our infancy with his providence, and our riper years with his wisdom and power; and to whose goodness I ask you to join with me in supplications that He will so enlighten the minds of your servants, guide their counsels, and prosper their measures, that whatsoever they do shall result in your good and shall secure to you the friendship and approbation of all nations."

That doesn't sound like an atheist to me!

The First Amendment to the United States Constitution:

"Congress shall make no law respecting an establishment of religion, or prohibiting the free exercise thereof; or abridging the freedom of speech, or of the press; or the right of the people peaceably to assemble, and to petition the Government for a redress of grievances."

How anyone can read the First Amendment and read into it that we can't have prayer in schools or display a nativity scene or the Ten Commandments on government property is beyond me. They definitely have a bigger imagination than I do!

The first line of the Amendment ("Congress shall make no law respecting an establishment of religion") is clearly to prohibit the establishment of a "state church", as with the "Church of England". The distorting of the first line of the Amendment to mean separation of church and state clearly violates the second line: "or prohibiting the free exercise thereof."

Our Founding Fathers knew that religion and the conscience of man could not and should not be legislated. Freedom of religion was the reason the early settlers came to the New World in the first place. They had foot prints on their necks when they got here! The thought of "separation of church and state" was not in their minds; they were Godly men and they built our country on Godly principles. Why would men of God who built a nation on Christian principles think the future leaders of that nation should be separated from God?

"We hold these truths to be self-evident, that all men are created equal, that they are endowed by their Creator with certain unalienable rights, that among these are Life, Liberty and the pursuit of Happiness."

Remove the Creator and where do our unalienable rights come from? From government?

That's a scary thought; sounds like Cuba.

CHAPTER
TWO

RELATIVISM

When I started writing this I had no intention of it being a 'Christian' book; it was to be a book on the state of our nation and our government. The more I read and research on the formation and workings of our government, the more I realize we cannot separate government and Christianity without destroying the government. Our Founding Fathers were Christian men who formed our government on Christian principles that can be traced right back to the Bible. The corner stone of the nation they built is the absolute moral truth of God that can **only** be found in the Holy Bible. Truth and morals based on anything else is relativism.

If you have trouble with the statement that truth and morals based on anything other than God's absolute moral truth being relativism, think of truth in the same manner as heat and light. They all have a negative counterpart. Cold and darkness do not exist; they are just the absence of heat and light. Same thing with a lie; it is just the absence of truth. If we reject God's absolute moral truth, whose definition of truth are we going to accept? Nancy Pelosi? Barney Frank? Maybe Obama will appoint a truth czar for us!

Over the years I have watched relativism at work. Relativism is very subtle and insidious in the way it reaches its tentacles into every part of our society, just as cancer spreads through the body. It reminds me of the arrow in the FEDEX logo, something that is right in front of your face all the time, but you never see it. Next time you see a FEDEX truck see if you can spot the arrow. (Hint: Quit looking at the letters and focus on the white space between the E and the X.) Once you spot the arrow, it is the first thing you see when you look at a FEDEX logo. It is the same with relativism. Once you recognize what it is, you see it all around you.

My dictionary defines relativism as, "a view that ethical truths depend on the individuals and groups holding them." In other words, truth can be whatever you want it to be, or there is no truth. With relativism everything becomes a "gray area." For Christians truth is from God and is absolute. God's truth is black and white; right is right and wrong is wrong. Once we get away from God's absolute moral truth, we have a lie. For example, look at the un-married young lady that finds she is pregnant and opts for an abortion. Now I believe in a woman's right to choose, but once she passes the point of conception, the choice has been made and we are no longer talking about choice, we're talking parental responsibility. The lie: If having a baby is inconvenient for the mother, she can kill her unborn child. With relativism, if the mother wants it to be true, it is. Once you remove God from the equation, you remove the reference point from which to determine right from wrong. Two wrongs ("Thou shall not kill" and "Thou shall not commit adultery") have never made a right and never will.

We see little lies all the time; like the sanitary landfill, it is still a garbage dump! Or co-habitation; it is still fornication! One thing about the truth of God is that it never needs to hide behind glossy terms; it can stand in the light of day! Whenever you see glossy terms and vagueness, it is a red flag for relativism and a lie. Big lies and little lies have one thing in common, they are both lies.

When we move into the political arena, we can find some really big lies. Hitler's Nazism was a Godless dictatorship built on lies and relativism. "Right" was defined as "What serves the state." They lied about their motives of world domination; they said God did not exist, and they lied about the value of human life, saying some people's life had more value than others. Does any of this sound familiar? We have no shortage of politicians telling us one thing and doing the opposite. They aren't telling us that God does not exist—yet, but they have made him irrelevant. And they are telling us that unborn babies, the old, and the sick have no value.

When Ronald Reagan was president, he spoke of Russia as the "Evil Empire" and took a lot of flak because of it. But, he spoke the truth and didn't gloss it over. Any nation that does not embrace Christianity is an evil empire at its core. I don't care if you are talking about Russia, China, North Korea, any of the Islamic Nations, or Hitler's Nazism. Even though they look different and speak different languages, they are all the same. They are all based on relativism and lies, and they all have the same goal; to overthrow Christianity and the United States of America. I remember in 1960 when Nikita Khrushchev, the Russian premier at the time, spoke at the United Nations General Assembly and made a grand impression by pounding his shoe on the podium. He made the statement, "We will defeat you without firing a shot; we will do it from within." For some reason, that statement has a lot more meaning to me now than it did then.

CHAPTER
THREE

SELF-GOVERNMENT

As Paul Harvey told us for decades, "Self government will not work without self discipline". Just what does the term 'self-government' mean? We hear of self- government, then go to the D.M.V. and get a $400 dose of government regulation along with one of those over the top of the glasses looks, and it is difficult to get a handle on self-government.

John Jay, one of the framers of the Constitution and first Chief Justice of the Supreme Court, said of the New York Constitution in 1777:

> *"From the people it must receive its spirit, and by them be quickened. Let virtue, honor, the love of liberty and science, be and remain the soul of the Constitution, and it will become the source of great and extreme happiness to this and future generations. Vice, ignorance, and a want of vigilance will be the only enemies that can destroy it. Against these provide, and of these be forever jealous. Every citizen ought diligently to read and study the Constitution of his country, and teach the rising generation to be free. By knowing their rights, they will sooner perceive*

*when they are violated, and be the better prepared to defend
and assert them.*

*Providence has given to our people the choice of their
rulers, and it is the duty, as well as the privilege and interest, of a Christian nation to select and prefer Christians
for their rulers."*

This quote of John Jay is from a book written in the 1850s.
It is interesting to note that if you go on-line to www.JohnJayin-
stitute.org and read his September, 1777 charge to the Grand Jury
of Ulster County, you find that the line "duty of a Christian nation
to select and prefer Christians for their rulers" has been omitted. A
book worm must have eaten it!

I know there are those who say that by selecting only Christians
as our leaders, we are being intolerant of other religions. No! That
is one of the lies that got us where we are. Tolerance is not the issue
here, liberty is. Christianity is the mortar that holds the bricks of
our nation together. The essence of Christianity is servitude. A
Christian is there to serve and has no power; the power comes
from God. We need the absolute moral truth in our government,
in the politicians, and in the political decisions they make. Don't
confuse intolerance with a Christian's refusal to water down his
faith. I will be tolerant of your beliefs, whatever they may be, and
you are welcome to reap the benefits that come from our Christian
based liberty. I just won't vote for you, unless you can convince
me your morals are based in God's absolute moral truth and not in
relativism. If a Christian compromises his beliefs, it doesn't show
me he is tolerant; it shows me how strong his beliefs are. I think
the Republican Party could also get a lot of mileage from that last
sentence.

We have all seen the Christian politician who goes to church
on Sunday and asks for the Lord's help in screwing everyone the
other six days of the week, and we will continue to see them.
They are no different than any other godless politician. They are

nothing more than wolves using Christianity as sheep's clothing. Our job as responsible voters is to discern the real from the phony, and we do that by paying attention to what they do and say, what they stand for, and their voting record. In short, take a good look at the fruit of the tree. It doesn't say much for the American voter when the best looking and smoothest talking candidate usually wins. I always like to see a candidate that can speak without a teleprompter. You know they are speaking the principals that are in their heart, and not worried about getting tripped up on lies they told yesterday or last week.

Self-government is nothing more than governing your self! That is the basis of our liberty and freedom. Self-government and freedom are not the right to do what we want; they are the right to do what is right without the government forcing us. It is our conscience, the inner force of moral restraint given by God. It is the "Golden Rule;" I don't want you to steal from me, so I won't steal from you. I don't want my wife to cheat on me, so I won't cheat on her. I don't want to be injured or killed by a drunk driver, so I won't drive drunk. Can you imagine the utopia we could be living in if everyone lived by the Golden Rule?

In California alone we could save close to seven billion dollars a year just by shutting down the prison system. Think of how much the government could be slashed. We wouldn't need traffic enforcement; the judicial system could be cut way back; all the social programs could be cut.

All of the laws that are passed are there to make up for the inability of society to love your neighbor as yourself and to do unto others as you would have them do unto you. The only reason you would have to lock your car would be to keep your friends from putting zucchini in it. I know—but it's nice to dream, isn't it. That is God's plan for us and the way it was in the beginning. We just haven't had the moral fortitude to hang onto it.

Seems like we are our own worst enemy!

For the gift of liberty our Founding Fathers gave us to survive, it is imperative the citizens of our great nation have personal honesty, integrity, the love of God and of their fellow man. The preservation of the family unit is absolutely essential to maintain our liberty. In a representative republic the power flows from the bottom up, it starts with you and me in the family. This is where the morality and the absolute moral truth of God, that is so vital to sustain our liberty, has to manifest itself. Gives a little deeper meaning to the phrase "The truth shall set you free," doesn't it?

Early on, any attempt to undermine the Christian moral base of our liberty met a brick wall and was dealt with surely and swiftly. An 1824 Pennsylvania Supreme Court decision upholding an indictment on blasphemy in favor of Christianity shows the importance our forefathers placed on protecting the moral underpinnings of our liberty. In part the court said:

> *"Even if Christianity was not part of the law of the land, it is the popular religion of the country, an insult on which would be indictable as directly tending to disturb the public peace. Christianity, general Christianity, is, and always has been, a part of the common law of Pennsylvania; not Christianity founded on particular religious tenets; not Christianity with an established Church, and tithes, and spiritual courts; but Christianity with liberty of conscience to all men. The first legislative act in the colony was the recognition of the Christian religion, and the establishment of liberty of conscience. It is called 'the Great Law' and is as follows— 'Where as the glory of Almighty God and the good of mankind is the reason and end of government, and therefore government itself is a venerable ordinance of God, and forasmuch as it is principally devised and intended by the Proprietary and Governor and freemen of Pennsylvania and territories there unto belonging, to make and establish such laws as shall best preserve true Christian and civil liberty, in opposition to all unchristian, licentious, and unjust practices, whereby God may have his due, Caesar his due, and the people their due.'*

'RESOLVED, therefore, that all persons living in this Province, who confess and acknowledge the one and Almighty and Eternal God to be the Creator, upholder, and ruler of the world, and who hold themselves obliged in conscience to live peaceably and justly in civil society, shall in no wise be molested.'

"Thus this wise legislature framed this great body of laws for a Christian country and a Christian people. Infidelity was then rare, and no infidels were among the first colonist. They fled from religious intolerance to a country where all were allowed to worship according to their own understanding."

"Every one had the right of adopting whatever opinion appeared to be the most rational concerning all matters of religious belief; thus securing by law this inestimable freedom of conscience, one of the highest privileges and greatest interest of the human race."

"Thus is the Christianity of the common law incorporated into the great law of Pennsylvania; and thus is it irrefragably proved that the laws and institutions of this state are built on the foundation of reverence for Christianity. On this the Constitution of the United States has made no alteration, nor in the great body of the laws, which was an incorporation of the common-law doctrine of Christianity, as suited to the condition of the colony, and without which no free government can long exist. Under the Constitution penalties against cursing and swearing have been enacted. If Christianity was abolished, all false oaths, all tests by oath in common form by the book, would cease to be indictable as perjury.

The thing that is most striking about this court perusal to me is that it is 180 degrees out from what is coming out of the courts today. Also, the last line is a heavy one. Remove God and there is no truth. Without truth, you could not prosecute perjury. Stop for a moment and ponder the ramification of that situation.

Surfing through the Supreme Court's past decisions one can see a definite pattern. From the birth of our nation until the 1890s, the courts came down on the side of Christianity and morality. In 1947 we had Everson vs. Board of Education that prevented parochial school students from riding on public school buses and in 1948 McCollum Vs Board of Education which prevented religious instruction on school property during the school day. This was the turning point and it has gone down hill from there.

How can this be? What happened?

CHAPTER
FOUR

RELATIVISM FILLS THE VACUUM

Horace Mann is known as the Father of Education and was instrumental in the establishment of the public school system in 1839. He accomplished a lot of great improvements for the education of our youth and rightfully earned a place in history. With all of the good things he was doing in education, no one seemed to notice that he left God behind. Instead of teaching the American philosophy of government, it was reduced to the fundamental concepts of the Constitution. The spirit of the Constitution was removed and only the letter remained. Before the advent of public schools, students learned how our representative republic is a better form of government than democracy.

After schools became organized under the state, the representative republic was discarded and democracy was taught. Democracy sounds great on the surface—the will of the people— but in reality it is nothing more than mob rule. Two wolves and a lamb voting on what's for dinner! Democracy is not a permanent form of government; it is just a stepping stone from representative republic to oligarchy.

Our Founding Fathers based the laws of our nation on scriptures such as Deuteronomy 4 thru 6 where God, as He was leading His chosen people to the Promised Land, gave His people the laws and decrees which they were to live by. We were told repeatedly in Deuteronomy to teach these laws and decrees to our children and to their children after them. We blew it! Remove God and relativism fills the vacuum.

Christian education was left to the churches and Sunday school. Nowadays there are a lot of the churches that don't even have Sunday school. I think teaching Christianity for an hour on Sunday morning creates an automatic disconnect. I can think back to my own experience with Sunday school and I suspect that most kids have the same thoughts, that this "God" stuff is optional and/ or secondary to "reading, writing, and global warming" because it's not mainstream in the everyday school curriculum. Also Sunday school is just Bible study with no connection between Christianity and the workings of our government.

Several generations after taking God out of the schools, we have godless people in our government appointing godless people to the Supreme Court, and a populace that is unaware of the importance of voting for Christians to fill these positions.

John Jay warned us; it is the duty of a Christian nation to select and prefer Christians for their rulers. As usual nobody was listening.

CHAPTER
FIVE

PROGRESSIVES

We have been conditioned over the years to think in terms of the two party system, the liberal left and the conservative right. Our country is divided right down the middle with the Republicans and Democrats throwing rocks at each other. That is what we are expected to keep doing, but there is another power at play here which started out working in the shadows and behind the scenes; with every success they quicken their pace and come further into the open. They are referred to as the progressives, statist, or secular far left radicals, and, while they pass themselves off as Democrat or Republican, their ideology doesn't really fit within or cross party lines. It's more like their ideology is outside party lines.

They are anti-God — government is their God — they believe government is supreme and can cure all our ills and fix all our problems including spending our money more wisely than we can. Christianity is the enemy! Their agenda can sucker a lot of people in when it is always packaged as, "It's for the children;" "It's to save the planet;" "It's a chicken in every pot;" and it always helps the down trodden and under privileged. They always make their agenda appeal to a person's self interest. Their programs always have the same results: they never work, they always need more money to make them work after they fail, and then they still don't work and need even more money. They always result in more government, and they always make the populace more dependent on government. And that is their objective; every step toward dependence is a step away from independence.

Our first progressive president was Theodore Roosevelt. Even though he was a Republican, he believed in separation of church and state, progressive income tax, promoted national health care and welfare, and was a conservationist, which on the surface all seem to be noble pursuits and appeal to most people's self interest. Trouble is they clash head-on with the founding principles of our nation.

The Tenth Amendment defines the division of power between the states and federal government: *"The powers not delegated to the United States by the Constitution, nor prohibited by it to the States, are reserved to the States respectively, or to the people."*

Our Founding Fathers knew the greatest threat to our representative republic was a centralized government, where the power is held by an elite few. That, after all is the definition of an oligarchy. To avoid the government from ever becoming centralized, the Founding Fathers placed checks and balances in the Constitution by establishing the three branches of government, the Legislative, Executive, and Judicial. In addition the Tenth Amendment limits the governing authority to the states. What can be done by the lower power should not be done by the higher. This enabled the federal government to carry out the tasks that the states could not do, but did not give it enough power to self-destruct.

James Madison summed it up well in Federalist #51:

> *"But what is government itself, but the greatest reflections on human nature? If men were angels, no government would be necessary. If angels were to govern men, neither external nor internal controls on government would be necessary. In framing a government which is to*

be administered by men over men, the great difficulty lies in this: you must first enable the government to control the governed; and in the next place oblige it to control itself."

After Theodore Roosevelt we have had a long succession of progressive presidents. I would venture to say that, with the exception of Ronald Reagan, they have all been progressive to some degree. Woodrow Wilson gave us the progressive income Tax in 1913. A very fitting name as it gave the progressives funding for their agenda and enabled the redistribution of wealth. This was not the first time the country had a progressive income tax. The first was to fund the Civil War and was repealed in 1872. Congress past another income tax in 1894 that was declared unconstitutional by the Supreme Court. Stephen Field, a thirty year veteran of the court, while repudiating Congress's action of passing a bill to tax a small voting bloc and exempting a larger bloc of voters also penned a prophecy:

"That a small progressive tax will be but the stepping stone to others, larger and more sweeping, till our political contests will become a war of the poor against the rich."

The Founding Fathers would have been appalled at even the thought of taxing one group of citizens and passing the benefits on to another group. Karl Marx would have felt right at home with it; one of his favorite slogans was: *"From each according to their ability, to each according to their needs."*

In Federalist #10 James Madison stated that:

"The apportionment of taxes on the various descriptions of property is an act which seems to require the most exact impartiality; yet there is, perhaps, no legislative act in which greater opportunity and temptation are given to a predominant party to trample on the rules of justice."

And trample on the rules of justice is exactly what the progressives did!

The progressive tax started with a top rate of 7% with no tax on married couples who made less than $4,000, which is the equivalent of about $85,000 today. Didn't take them long to fulfill Field's prophecy. By the time Herbert Hoover left office, the top rate was up to 63%. Franklin Roosevelt put it up to 90%. Roosevelt was practicing on a large scale what Field called "The war of the rich against the poor" and Madison called "the spirit of party and faction".

During the Great Depression the progressives started America on a course that we are still on today. With the aid of a democratic majority in congress, Roosevelt was able to pass laws and create administrative agencies at a frightening pace. He used taxation to redistribute wealth by creating welfare, public works, pension, and unemployment programs. He created electoral constituencies of unions, senior citizens, farmers, and used the treasury to reward his friend's with subsidies and punish his opponents with audits.

In the 1936 presidential race Roosevelt used the different agencies of government to dole out subsidies for votes; the Republican opponent could not even hope to match his money. Roosevelt defeated the Republican Alf Landon by an electoral vote of 523 to 8.

The Supreme Court fought back at first, declaring that the "New Deal" programs exceeded the Constitutional authority by violating private property rights and states sovereignty. Roosevelt was able to replace some older justices with new justices that shared his views. That not being enough, he increased the court from seven to nine justices. It was not long before the court was little more than his "lap dog".

The policies and agenda of the progressives are a full frontal assault on our liberty and freedom. They have breached the checks and balances placed in the Constitution by the Founding Fathers. The result of Roosevelt's and the progressives programs was to make the depression the "Great Depression" and to put our nation on the road to tyranny.

Franklin Roosevelt was the first progressive president to have a progressive majority in Congress. The second was Lyndon Johnson, who gave us the war on poverty and the "Great Society". The third is the present Obama administration, with Harry Reid, Nancy Pelosi, and friends who are taking us down the road to tyranny at a dizzying pace.

The progressives are no longer in the shadows; they are out in the open and in your face. We are so far down the road to tyranny that we are no longer a representative republic. I would describe our government as being a "smiley face socialism" and as soon as we pass the point where we the people do not have the power to turn it around, the smiley face will disappear. And the bills that can push us past that point are in Congress right now with the "cap and trade" and "nationalized heath care"!

I am of the opinion that the 2010 Congressional election will be our last chance to take our nation back and return to our founding principles. By the time Obama has four years in office, he will be as firmly entrenched as FDR was in 1936 and will have made enough people dependent on government that we will have more voters collecting entitlements and government paychecks than voters paying taxes.

He will be buying votes with tax payer's money. Actually he is already buying votes. Of the $158 billion of the stimulus money released so far, most has gone to Connecticut, New York, New Jersey, and California, all blue states. In the counties that supported Obama during the election there was roughly $69 per person of stimulus money. In counties that supported John McCain, there was $34 per person.

White House spokesman Robert Gibbs insists that no politics are involved and he is right. No one is actually directing funds to Obama supporters and away from McCain supporters. It has been built in the system since the Roosevelt administration. The money goes to those that support big government.

We need to throw every progressive out and elect people whose first concern is the survival of our liberty and freedom.

Instead of electing these eggheads that are educated beyond their intelligence, I would like to see the halls of Congress packed with unemployed loggers from the Pacific Northwest. My reasoning behind that thought is that every one of them owns an axe and knows how to use it!

CHAPTER
SIX

RIGHT WING EXTREMIST?

I know that by now I have labeled myself as a right wing extremist to many of you. Let's take a closer look at the term "right wing extremist". I think the first image that pops into most peoples mind is a "skin head" Neo-Nazi with tattoos, combat boots and a chain drive wallet who goes around beating up Jews and Blacks. I confess to being a skin head, but that is because of my genes, not my ideology.

When we describe someone as being a left or right extremist, we are describing where that individual stands in the political spectrum of government between anarchy, which is no government, and totalitarianism, which is complete government control.

Some sources mistakenly argue that Nazism and Totalitarianism are on the far right of the political spectrum. My dictionary defines Totalitarianism as: "The political concept that the citizen should be totally subject to an absolute state authority." How can we be subject to absolute state authority on the far right? In anarchy there is no government.

Nazism is a totalitarian type of government, so that puts the skin head on the far left of the political spectrum. Since government tapers off to nothing on the extreme right we will find that area virtually unpopulated. Moving a little bit left from the extreme right, we find those who want to limit government; these are the real "right wing extremist". In this group we will find people like George Washington, John Adams, Thomas Jefferson, James Madison, Alexander Hamilton, Benjamin Franklin, John Jay, just to name a few. I would feel honored to be labeled as a right wing extremist.

I am not aware of anyone who is trying to move our government to the right of where the Founding Fathers were. If you are of the opinion that anyone who is trying to move our government back to the founding principals is a right wing extremist, I think you should stand back, take a good look at your position and think it through. It is not just the destruction of my liberty and freedom that you are aiding and abetting; it is also yours and your children's. The so called right wing extremist are the ones who are leaving skid marks with their heels, trying to prevent the secular far left from dragging us into totalitarianism. The only extremists we have are the secular far left. The right wing extremist is nonexistent, nothing but a smoke screen from those on the far left trying to divert the attention from themselves.

Over the years there has been a steady movement to the left and towards totalitarianism. In 1964 when I cast my first vote, I was in the mainstream of the Republican Party. Today, even though I am still standing in the same spot, the Republican Party is off to my left! The Republican Party today is further left than the Democratic Party of the early 60s.

The progressives are very talented with the smoke and mirrors, and if you are not on their side of an issue, they are quick to label you as a "hick from the sticks" or a "right wing extremist". Their standard mode of operation is to create division, with neither faction ever winning. The only winner is the progressives with the populace more dependent on government and more government agencies. They never let a good crisis go to waste; every crisis is an opportunity for another government agency. A good example is the Department of Energy. It was created in 1977 during the Carter administration with the sole propose of lessening our dependence on foreign oil after the oil crisis of the 70s. 32 years later we have an agency with 16,000 employees, 100,000 contract employees, and a budget of 24.2 billion a year. And we are now more dependent on foreign oil than we were in 1977. If government had just stayed out of the way, we could have been free from foreign oil in the 80's, would have saved billions upon billions of dollars, and would have had 116,000 more people pulling the wagon instead of riding in it. Every government agency has a similar scenario and track record.

I don't know who I am the most upset with, the small percentage of our population who are systematically destroying our country or the large percentage of citizens who are either helping with the destruction, through ignorance, or sitting there with their head where the sun don't shine and letting it happen. Where is the outrage?

Where is the outrage with all the czars that are being created almost on a daily basis? We are literally being "czared and feathered" and no one seems to care. We have more Czar's than the Romanov Dynasty. Does it bother any one besides me that we have a quasi government in place right now that answers to no one but the President? This is centralized government at its finest.

Our capitalist free market economy has created more happiness and prosperity for more people than any other system of government since the beginning of mankind. America is the country that "the tired, the poor, the huddled masses yearning to breathe free," flocked to by the tens of thousands. They left family and friends behind and gambled everything they had on just the hope of being free. America was the hope of the world. Where will they go when we become a nation of bearded bicyclists with B.O.?

America was built by God's people with God's guiding hand to be the "Shining City on the Hill" for the oppressed of the world and for other countries of the world to emulate. If America fails we will be just another country, just like the countries that the huddled masses left behind, and Satan will have won this round in the war of good vs. evil.

Have you noticed how the talking heads on TV never mention the war of good vs. evil? They will allude to it and nibble around the edges, but with the exception of a few pastors, they never come right out and say it. As soon as you mention the war of good and evil the progressives are on you like a duck on a June bug and paint you in the same light as the cross-eyed guy with no front teeth who was abducted by aliens and taken for a ride in the spaceship.

The secular anti-God crowd has been throwing monkey wrenches in the gears of our government and economy since the birth of our nation to get us to the point we are today. Who else but Satan could or would orchestrate an assault on our country of this magnitude over a two hundred year time span? Remove God and evil fills the vacuum.

The secular left does not believe in God; government is their god and Barack Obama Is the current messiah. The only resemblance I have noticed between Obama and God is that neither seems to have a birth certificate. There is evil in this world and a lot of it is in the leadership of our country. We have to stop thinking left and right, liberal and conservative and start thinking vertical. Is this coming from God or Satan? When I hear our leaders in Washington talking, I hear the same voice I heard in 1960 when Nikita Khrushchev said "We will defeat you without firing a shot, we will do it from within".

Am I accusing every one on the left of being evil? No, I am not; there are some who are evil, but I will leave that judgment to God. Most are just pawns being manipulated and used by the progressives. There are a lot of people that are bellied-up to the public feed trough with entitlements, government jobs, and welfare that are voting to keep their personal gravy train rolling. They do not realize that their only security is in their ability to perform and that the progressives are buying their votes to further the progressive agenda. There are also a lot of people who are compassionate and truly feel the wealth and justice should be distributed more evenly. They have bought into the Marxist philosophy "From each according to his ability, to each according to his need" without realizing wealth redistribution turns ability into a liability and need into an asset. There are still others who vote with their emotions and rational thought never enters the picture. These are the people standing on the fantail of the Titanic saying, "My, doesn't the quartet sound superb."

In short I think all of them are ignorant of what makes this country great and what makes it free. And why shouldn't they be? It hasn't been taught in our schools for over a hundred years! Let's face it, life is not fair! We are created equal, but we are not equal. Some people are smarter than others and make sacrifices and wise decisions. Some just work harder than others; some are just plain lucky and some are all of the above. If government would just stay out of the way, even the stupid and lazy can support themselves with a higher standard of living than a totalitarian government will give them.

CHAPTER
SEVEN

ENEMIES: FOREIGN AND DOMESTIC

Ever since Franklin Roosevelt packed the Supreme Court with secular activist judges, we have never been free of them and have lost the strongest and most effective of the checks and balances placed in the Constitution by the Founding Fathers. As long as we keep re-electing progressives for president and to Congress, who appoint progressive judges, we never will be free of them. Thomas Jefferson said in a letter to William Jarvis on Sept 28, 1820: *"You seem to consider the judges as the ultimate arbiters of all Constitutional questions; a very dangerous doctrine indeed, and one which would place us under the despotism of an oligarchy."*

An excellent example of what happens when you have godless activist judges on the bench is the 1985 Supreme Court ruling on Wallace vs. Jaffree where the Court prohibited a daily moment of silence in public school classrooms. It is interesting to read the Alabama District Court ruling that was overturned in the Supreme Court:

> *"The drafters of the First Amendment understood the First Amendment to prohibit the federal government only from establishing a national religion. Anything short of*

the outright establishment of a national religion was not seen as violative of the First Amendment. For example, the federal government was free to promote various Christian religions and expend monies in an effort to see that those religions flourished. This was not seen as violating the establishment clause. (R. Cord, Separation of Church and State 1982)."

"But even President Jefferson signed into law bills which provided federal funds for the propagation of the gospel among the Indians. Based upon the historical record Professor Cord concludes that Jefferson, even as President, did not interpret the establishment clause to require complete independence from religion in government."

"One thing which becomes abundantly clear after reviewing the historical record is that the founding fathers of this country and the framers of what became the First Amendment never intended the establishment clause to erect an absolute wall of separation between the federal government and religion. Through the chaplain system, the money appropriated for the education of Indians, and the Thanksgiving proclamations, the federal government participated in secular Christian activities.

From the beginning of our country, the high and impregnable wall which Mr. Justice Black referred to in Everson vs. Board of Education, 330 U.S. 1, 18 67 S.Ct504, 513, 91 L.Ed. 711 (1947), was not as high and impregnable as Justice Black's revisionary literary flourish would lead one to believe."

"The real object of the First Amendment was not to countenance, much less to advance Mohammedanism, or Judaism, or infidelity, by prostrating Christianity, but to exclude all rivalry among Christian sects (denominations) and to prevent any national ecclesiastical patronage of the national government."(quoting Justice Joseph Story)

Can't let little things like facts and legal precedent get in the way when we have an agenda, can we?

If the polls that say 84% of Americans consider themselves Christian are right, why are we electing godless people to lead us? How many of the so called Christians have fallen prey to relativism and are not really Christians at all? How many Christians voted for a candidate that supports abortion or same sex marriage? We all have to ask ourselves, "Is my vote helping this nation to be a Christian nation or helping our nation down the path of relativism?" Just as a blind person who has never seen light can not recognize darkness, our secular leaders who have never seen the absolute moral truth of God can not recognize the nature of evil. Without God we have no reference point between right and wrong

When our elected representatives, both the president and Congress are sworn into office, they take an oath with their hand on the Holy Bible. Part of that oath is that they swear to protect us from enemies both foreign and domestic. That is their duty. Trouble is they are our number one domestic enemy! With the activist judges they appoint along with the laws and policies they pass, they are aiding and abetting the growth of relativism.

As I write this, the financial situation looks pretty bleak. Companies going broke, housing market in the tank; most people have lost about 40% of their retirement savings and the unemployment rate is climbing. Just heard on the news that the only employment sector that is growing is- you guessed it- government jobs!

Thomas Jefferson said: *"My reading of history convinces me that most bad government results from too much government."*

I get the impression that most Americans are of the opinion that in order for us to lose our freedom and liberty, there has to be some sort of a military coup to overthrow the government; something similar to what happened in Cuba when Castro took over or the Bolshevik Revolution in Russia. That is one way it could happen, but it isn't the only way. Actually it's much easier than that. Like the old saying "All it takes for evil to prevail is for good men to do nothing". All we have to do is sit here and watch the government grow and take more and more control of our lives like we have been doing, and it **will** happen. The only difference between anarchy and a dictatorship is the amount of control the government has over the people. In anarchy there is zero government control; with a dictator there is 100% control. The question is, "How much control is the American people going to let the government take before they wakeup and say 'Enough'?"

We are in a very similar situation as Germany was in the late 1920s and early 1930s. The German people waited too long and those that finally protested were shot. I don't know exactly where that point of no return is, but I do know that when I see legislation like HR45, hate crime legislation, fairness doctrine, cap and trade, and national healthcare coming down the pike, I start to get nervous. If you think the same thing that happened to Germany can't happen to us — get in touch with me, I can make you a hell of a deal on a bridge...

Our legislators, both state and federal, are busy pushing through legislation for special interest groups and bringing home the bacon for their constituents. This is good to insure their re-election, but there is no apparent thought given to the welfare of "the goose that laid the golden egg," and they are plucking it to death! And this is not all the fault of politicians. A lot of the blame can be laid at the feet of the voters. I think the whole nation is suffering from FLS (Free Lunch Syndrome). We send our representatives to Washington with the instructions to rip off the rest of the nation for all you can get and send it home to us! The purpose of the federal government is to do the things for the states that cannot be done on the state level, like national security, maintaining the infrastructure, and regulating what must be regulated.

The United States has more enemies in this world than friends. It does not appear that our leaders even know who our enemies are, let alone understand their ideologies and what to do about them. We have been wallowing around in a fog of ignorance for decades, without understanding the goals and mindset of our enemies. The United Nations is full of communist, socialist, and totalitarian godless governments that all have the same goal, world domination. The only thing standing in their way of world domination is the United States of America. Instead of the United States of America being the "Shining City on a Hill" promoting freedom and equality for all, our leaders seem to be doing all they can to help our enemies defeat us!

Just look at our trade practice with China. We have mega-sized container ships bringing ship loads of Chinese products to be sold in the U.S., then turn around and go back to China empty to get another load. I have no problem with trading with China, but I do have a problem with the trade deficit. It is just plain stupid, almost as stupid as giving them the Panama Canal. It is a noble thought to help a neighbor pursue a peaceful economic development, but as long as it is a Communist government, the peace will only last until they perceive they are stronger than the United States.

All we are doing is helping them become a super power capable of coming back and biting us. I suppose it's a waste of time to worry about that. With as much as we are borrowing from China, they will own us first. With all the money China is making from doing our manufacturing for us, they are loaning it back to us and buying up oil and mineral rights all over the world.

Our leaders seem to be especially naive in dealing with the Islamic nations. And the Islamic nations seem to be more than willing to capitalize on their naivety. Muslims have the world divided into two groups—them and the infidels. Jihad (holy war) is a religious duty; Islam is under obligation to conquer the world. Jihad does not end until all infidels are either converted to Islam or dead. That doesn't leave a lot of wiggle room for peaceful co-existence with them. Again the peace will only last as long as they are in a position of weakness. I agree that it is good to be good neighbors and expose their population to our liberty and freedom. The inalienable rights of life, liberty, and the pursuit of happiness were made available by God to all men. The United States of America is the only country that has laid claim to those rights. We have an obligation to be the "Shining City on a Hill" to give hope for the oppressed people of the world, but we have to realize when dealing with totalitarian types of governments that we are dealing with evil regimes that want to bury us. I think Teddy Roosevelt had the right philosophy: "Speak softly and carry a big stick."

I can't say how many times we have watched the same scene play out between Israel and Hamas. The Arabs bomb Israel with either rockets or a suicide bomber in a market place or a bus and kill a bunch of innocent people. Israel tries all of the diplomatic channels that do no good. After they take it as long as they can, they retaliate and kick the Arabs butts, then somebody negotiates a cease fire. In the news the Israelites are always portrayed as the aggressors, and we hear the sob stories of all the innocent Palestinian women and children that were killed in the Israel attack. As soon as Hamas regroups and rearms, we have a repeat performance. No doubt Hamas will make good use of the 900 million of our tax dollars that Hillary passed on to them after the last attack.

They just keep coming back and will continue to do so as long as there is a breath in them, just like Osama bin Laden will come out of whatever cave he is hiding in as soon as it is safe. Just like the atheist will keep pushing until it is illegal to mention God in our country. Just like homosexuals will keep on until they have same sex marriage and destroy the family structure. There is evil in this world and there will be until Jesus Christ returns and puts an end to it. Winston Churchill said of truth: *"You can resent it, ignore it, deride, or distort it—but there it is!"*

It is the duty of every American and every Christian to demand that our leaders base their decisions and policies on the moral truth of God. Some will say, "I am not a Christian"! That is fine, and it is your choice. But you are living in a Christian country enjoying the fruits of our Christian liberty; you had best understand where that liberty comes from. Even if you are not a Christian, the framers of our constitution were and they gave us a form of government that is based on Christian law to hold the government in check and protect the people from government. Our system of government requires that the citizens have personal honesty, integrity, and live by Gods laws. ***Our government has no protection from corrupt and unscrupulous politicians other than the watchful eye of its citizens.***

The soul of our nation is the sum of the souls of the people. If the soul of our nation is standing on the street corner smoking pot, listening to rap crap on an I-pod, we are in deep do-do!

Our Founding Fathers had a clean slate to work with. They could have given us any form of government. There were some who wanted to give us an oligarchy and make George Washington our king. That was and still is the most common form of government, where the power is held by an elite few. The liberty and freedom of the people are whatever the elite few allow the people to have. Our representative republic is just the opposite; the power is held by the people and the power of the government is whatever the people allow it to have. Over the last eighty years, we the people have let government run wild and obtain tremendous power. Somewhere there is a point of no return where we automatically become an oligarchy, and it is my fear, that we are dangerously close to that point. In our entitlement prone, rob-Peter-to-pay-Paul society, once we have more Paul's than Peter's, it's all over. If we are going to save our freedom and liberty, it is now or never!

CHAPTER
EIGHT

ENVIRONMENTAL MOVEMENT

I can recall reading a statement that has stuck with me since the environmental movement first started gaining momentum, "If you want to control a nation's economy control its natural resources". You can look back over the last 30 or 40 years and see how every one of our nation's natural resources have been shut down in the name of the environment. You can go right down the list; mining, oil, logging, commercial fishing, agriculture have all been regulated so heavily that only mega corporations can stand a chance of eking out a profit. For the most part we are buying from other countries that have little or no concern for the environment, and less for the well being of the United States of America.

I am a firm believer of being good stewards of this little blue ball we call home. If all this regulation is for the protection of the earth's environment, wouldn't it make more sense to keep these industries at home where we have control on the environmental effects? Or is the environmental movement being used as a political ploy to gain power and control over the nation's economy? The industrial might of the United States of America has effectively been shut down and our economy has become a service oriented economy. When times get tough, like right now, and people don't have the cash, the first thing they do is stop buying services they can't afford. The economy spirals downward, and, without the industrial base, we have no way to turn the economy around again. But fear not, the government will save us! All it will cost you is your liberty and freedom.

I have doubted the global warming agenda right from the start; the first thing that raised my suspicion was that it had been less than ten years since we were hearing about global cooling. The second thing to arouse my suspicion is that we never hear any specific numbers as to how much global warming we have in a given number of years. The only numbers I have been able to find, after a lot of looking, are one degree in the last 150 years and two-tenths of a degree C in the last seventy years.

Neither one of those numbers make me tremble in fear, especially since the last ten years the globe has been cooling to the point that Al Gore has quit calling it global warming and is now calling it climate change!

Another problem I have is with the weather stations where the temperature data is collected. Since planet Earth does not have a tongue to stick a thermometer under, we have to rely on thousands of weather stations scattered around the globe. Are all of these weather stations in the same spot they were in 20, 30, 50 or 75 years ago? If not they can not give an accurate history of the temperature in one specific location. Even for the ones that are still in the original location, is the environment around it still the same, or is what used to be a cow pasture 20 years ago now an asphalt parking lot on the sunny side of a concrete building. There is an abundance of issues that cloud the accuracy of the temperature data, such as the change of the type of paint on the white louvered boxes that house the thermometers, which accounted for about half of the global warming temperature change. And, just by coincidence, the change in paint took place right at the start of the global warming panic. Another big jump in global temperature in the early 1990s just happened to coincide with the break-up of the Soviet Union when Russia decided they had more important things to do than maintain weather stations in Siberia.

Doesn't take a rocket scientist to figure out there are no accurate historical records of global temperature. It was done with computer programs. Which brings up the question of who programmed the computer, and what was the agenda? Whatever agenda you want, you can get just by carefully selecting what year to use as a base year. 1860, when the little ice age started its decline and 1966 the coldest Arctic year ever recorded seem to be the popular base years for the global warming crowd. If you prefer global cooling, go for the 1930s. Makes you wonder what possible motive all of these so called scientists could have which would cause them to resort to junk science and perpetuate the global warming hoax. You don't suppose the six billion of our tax dollars that is dumped into their feed trough every year could have any influence on their research, do you?

Then you have to ask yourself why is our government spending six billion a year for global warming research?

The 2009 International Conference on Climate Change was recently held in New York. There were over 70 scientists expressing the view that global warming is not a crisis, a view shared by over 30,000 of their colleagues. As expected, the mainstream media basically ignored it. One of the leading speakers was European Union and Czech Republic President Vaclav Klaus, who is one of most outspoken critics in Europe of the theory of man-made global warming. He said:

> *"The global warming alarmists are like the communist of old Europe. The communist did not listen to opposing views; they didn't even try to argue back. They considered you a naïve, uninformed, and confused person, an eccentric complainer. It is very similar now." Klaus concluded his speech with: "The environmentalist speak about saving*

*the planet. We have to ask—from what? And from whom?
I think I know for sure, we have to save the planet, and us,
from them"*

We already see activity in the U.N. and from some of our politicians that is moving towards establishing an international tribunal to regulate carbon emissions. We are hearing talk and seeing T.V. commercials about cap and trade. If "cap and trade legislation" gets passed you can kiss your liberty goodbye! The government will be able to control our every action through taxation, from the use of fossil fuels to cow flatulence!

I think they use that six dollar F-word so the down home good ol'e boys that have a diet of beans, beer and pickled eggs won't catch-on that they will tax farts!

Cap and trade will give them complete control of our economy and therefore our sovereignty. Makes me wonder if the elected officials, who are sworn to uphold our constitution and protect us from enemies, both foreign and domestic, who are pushing cap and trade legislation, should be tried for treason. (That should get a black helicopter hovering over my house.) Seems like the American people will buy anything that is packaged in environmental baloney and tied up with a green ribbon.

CHAPTER
NINE

CHRISTIANITY

The battle for our liberty and religious freedom is an on-going battle; it did not end with the conclusion of the Revolutionary War. Each generation has to answer the call to preserve liberty for the next generation. We have had several generations of Christians that have failed miserably in answering that call. We have allowed God to be pushed out of the schools. Our children are being fed a diet of relativism and the truth of God is not in them.

I know there are exceptions and that statement sounds harsh. I would recommend you check out The Barna Group web site www. barna.org. and look at the research they have done; it is down right scary. We have a tsunami of kids coming onto adulthood that make their decisions on the world view instead of God's truth. Their views on abortion, homosexuality, lying, and general personal integrity has relativism written all over them. Wait until they start running for political office!

Christianity has been neutralized; it has become a spineless, toothless social club where we go to church on Sunday and worry about our personal salvation. We have bought into the lie of separation of church and state. How many pastors fold up when their tax exempt status is threatened by the ACLU after saying something political from the pulpit? It's high time for all the churches to rise up in unity and in one voice tell the ACLU to sit down and shut-up!

Christianity has been watered down and diluted over the years. In colonial times there were just a handful of Christian denominations; now there are thousands of different Christian churches all claiming to teach the truth of the Bible and the message of Jesus Christ. Yet, no two of them can agree enough on the message to worship God together under the same roof. Is this from God? I don't think so; I think I see the tracks of relativism. All Christian denominations have the truth of God in their teaching. It's mostly a matter of degree of how much truth they have. Most people seem to select the church they attend the same way they select which politician they vote for; they go for the warm fuzzy feeling and pay little attention to doctrine and what they stand for.

I have seen the different denominations compared to a very old and beautiful stained glass window. Over the years some of the original panes have been broken and lost and have been replaced with clear glass. Much of the original beauty has been lost. In some denominations you can hardly recognize what the original was. How are we to sort through all the confusion and find the truth of God?

I am reminded of the game we used to play way back when; if I remember right I think they called it 'Telephone." Every one would sit in a circle around the room. The first person would whisper a message in the ear of the second person, the second person would whisper it to the third, and on around the room. The last person would give the message out loud and whoever was "it," tried to guess what the original message was. The only place you can be sure of getting the original message is from the first person.

We need to go back to the early church fathers, study their writings to see what they believed. If your church doesn't look anything like theirs, I for one would be asking, "Why?" Jesus said, "I AM". He did not say I AM whatever you want me to be!

To accept Jesus Christ as our Lord and Savior is the first step in becoming a Christian and can be compared to scrubbing a dirty white wall in your kitchen. Once you start, there is no place to stop! Some haven't got past the first swipe on their wall, I don't mean to sound self-righteous. In fact, I just counted 22 pictures and placards on my kitchen wall. Please, do not look behind the pictures! We all face the same struggle in our journey to follow in Jesus' footsteps we take a few steps forward and find we are out of our comfort zone, then take a step back. Every day we are faced with the choice, "Am I taking a step forward or backward?" The environment we are in has a lot of influence on whether we step forward or back. Am I in a small rural community where I am known to everyone around me? Everywhere I look do I see friends of my parents, relatives and neighbors, or am I just another face in the crowd on a busy city street where the only ones that will make eye contact are the drug dealers and prostitutes?

Our Founding Fathers wore their Christian faith like a suit of clothes; their faith went with them every where they went all week long. Their faith was not just a Sunday "thing". It was incorporated into their work, their relationships, their schools, their civic affairs, their home life, their Saturday night social events, and their whole being.

CHAPTER
TEN

THE EROSION OF MORALITY

We have to realize that the constant attack on our American Christian heritage is meant to destroy the power of God and establish the rule of man. *We are in a war of ideologies and the battle ground is morality.* I think the forces that are constantly attacking our Christian heritage and pulling us towards relativism is the same force that drew Eve to the tree in the middle of the garden. This is the spiritual warfare between good and evil that those Bible thumpers keep talking about!

It is becoming all too apparent what happens when our society gets cut loose from its moral anchor. We have homosexuals parading in the streets demanding equal rights to marry their same sex partners. They even try to equate their movement with the Civil Rights of the 1960s. They already have equal rights for a man to marry a woman or a woman to marry a man just like the rest of us. It is not a civil rights issue; it is a moral issue. They are demanding the additional right to remove the legal and moral restraints on their sexual perversion.

You may notice that I never use the term 'gay' in reference to the homosexual life style. I am not a very politically correct person and I resent the fact that the homosexual crowd has bastardized a perfectly good word from our language that in no way reflects their life style. I am using a lot of restraint in referring to them as homosexuals.

Political correctness has robbed our society of its self-cleansing mechanism. There was a time that when a sexual pervert rode into town, he got tarred and feathered, then rode out of town on a rail! I don't advocate that type of action, but, you have to admit, it was effective. I believe in the "love the sinner-hate the sin" approach. Loving the sinner and hating the sin is a very thin line to walk; if we veer off to either side we are in dangerous territory. When we love the sinner, without hating the sin, we are in effect putting our stamp of approval on the sin. If we veer off on the other side to hate the sin without loving the sinner, we are forgetting the fact that we are all sinners.

I am as guilty of this as anyone, but believe me, I am changing my ways!

We need to speak up when confronted with something that goes against our values. Not standing up for our values is just about the same as not having any. For example:

When a friend or relative comes for a weekend visit with their "significant other" and wants to go to bed together in your home, with your children present, do you tell them they either sleep in separate rooms or get a motel?

It is so easy to look the other way and remain silent for fear of hurting their feelings or offending them. They should be told, in no uncertain terms, that you find their actions offensive. If they are offended by that, oh well, you might as well both be offended. Stand up for your values! Political correctness be damned!

I realize that I am an old fogey who is out of touch with the values of the more enlightened younger generation, but I would like to point out that I've been there and done that and that God's laws are the same yesterday, today, and forever! There was a time people at least had the decency to sneak!

Anyone who stands up for the sanctity of marriage is called an intolerant hatemonger, bigot, and homophobe. We saw an example of the homosexual crowd's "tolerance" after Prop 8 passed in California. Call me what you will, but I draw my moral "line in the sand" at the Ten Commandments. My moral values are firmly rooted in the Judeo-Christian tradition. Those values tell me that homosexuality is a perversion.

1) Leviticus 18:22: "Do not lie with a man as one lies with a woman; that is detestable."

2) Romans 1:26-27: "Because of this, God gave them over to shameful lusts. Even their women exchanged natural relations for unnatural ones. In the same way the men also abandoned natural relations with women and were inflamed with lust for one another. Men committed indecent acts with other men, and received in themselves the due penaltyfor their perversion."

3) 1Corinthians 6:9: "Do you not know that the wicked will not inherit the kingdom of God? Do not be deceived: Neither the sexually immoral nor idolaters nor adulterers nor male prostitutes nor homosexual offenders nor drunkards nor slanderers nor swindlers will inherit the kingdom of God."

4) Jude 7: "In a similar way, Sodom and Gomorrah and the surrounding towns gave themselves up to sexual immorality and perversion. They serve as an example of those who suffer the punishment of eternal fire."

Where do the homosexuals draw a line in the sand and say "on the other side of that line is immoral?" And don't pass over that question too fast; stop and give it some thought.

It never ceases to amaze me how mankind can be drawn away from the word of God. It is a reoccurring theme that has been taking place since the time of Adam and Eve and the original sin. In all other areas of knowledge man can pick up what previous generations have learned and build upon it. When it comes to following the truth of God, it's like Will Rodgers said: "Most folks have to stick their finger in the light socket." You can see it all through the Bible, through the history of our nation, and you can see it all around you today. Man always has a better way until he paints himself in a corner and is confronted with a problem that has no human solution. Then he turns to God and starts the cycle over again. I came across this little tidbit of wisdom right after I pulled my finger out of the light socket.

Have you ever wondered why homosexuals are not content with a civil union in which they can have the legal rights of a married couple, but they demand the rights of traditional marriage? It is because the homosexual-right-to-marry agenda is not really about homosexuals at all. They are just pawns in the bigger war, the spiritual war between good and evil, with the objective of destroying the family unit.

The sad part is that most Americans don't even realize we are in a war and it is very near to being lost. Homosexuals have already won over the courts. They have infiltrated the schools and are teaching their perverted life style to our children. They have come a long way since 1960 when homosexual conduct was a felony in all 50 states. Prop 8 in California passed 52% to 48%. What will it be in the next go around? I have heard it said many times: As California goes, so goes the nation.

Homosexuality is just one front where the exclusion of God has affected our moral values.

God has been removed from our schools, news media, government, and entertainment. We now have a couple of generations who have been raised with relative morals. Relative to what? How you feel or peer pressure from your friends? Moral values have to be anchored in solid truth; they can't be floating around depending on how you feel today.

The schools are rewriting history to fit their agenda, the news media is telling us what they want us to hear, politicians are doing what it takes to insure their re-election and fill their pockets, with no regard to what is best for the nation.

The entertainment industry has turned into a cesspool. I remember when Red Skelton used to end his TV program with

"Good Night and God Bless." His programs were funny and clean. Now all of the sitcoms are promoting promiscuous life styles, either homosexual or unmarried sex and filthy language. The dramas are all about how many people can be maimed or killed and how many buildings can be blown up before the next commercial. All because God has been taken out of the picture, and there is no foundation under their morals.

In 1939 the movie 'Gone With The Wind' hit the big screen. It was a real affront on common decency when Clark Gable said "Frankly, my dear, I don't give a damn!"

Doesn't take long in front of the T.V. to see how far we have slid down the moral scale.

We can watch the old reruns of *Leave It to Beaver* or *Ozzie and Harriet* and I think most of us would agree they were pretty corny. Do we have to let our morals go down the tubes, just to keep from being corny?

The soul of our nation is a sum of the souls of the people. If we are a Christian people, our nation is a Christian nation. If we embrace moral relativism and reject God by rejecting His absolute moral truth, we remove the cornerstone our nation was built upon and become a godless people and a godless nation that is headed down the road to socialism and eventually a dictatorship.

I have heard the adage in Christian circles for years that "coincidence is when God wants to remain anonymous". I believe there is a lot of truth in it, but there is also a dark flipside to it. Coincidence can also be when Satan wants to remain anonymous, and Satan always wants to remain anonymous.

When we stand back and take a good look at the big picture over the last 200+ years, we see a definite pattern of events. The Christian principles and our liberty have been systematically peeled away, silently and insidiously, just like peeling an onion, one layer at a time over ten or twelve generations. It started with taking the Bible out of the classroom; then after public schools were established, God was taken out of the curriculum. Instead of the importance of God's absolute moral truth in our representative republic being taught, democracy and relativism entered the classroom. After a couple of generation's of godless education, we see godless people showing up on the political arena and in the courts.

Once we have godless judges we have court decisions against Christianity and morality, and the homosexuals started their march out of the closet into our classrooms, churches, media, and entertainment, causing the breakup of moral values and the family unit. We have corrupt self-serving politicians making immoral laws and policies and a constant growth in government which is slowly taking our freedom and liberty.

We have all kinds of division in our society, white vs. black, Democrat vs. Republican, rich vs. poor, Christian vs. non-Christian, citizen vs. government, and on and on.

Is this all mere coincidence, or is it a plan systematically being carried out over a 200 year period? They don't call Satan the great deceiver for nothing.

CHAPTER
ELEVEN

THE GREATEST GENERATION

My parent's generation is known as The Greatest Generation and they had a different set of values than what you see in our society today. They had personal honesty and integrity; a man could shake your hand, give you his word, and you could go to the bank with it.

They came from tough stock; most of their parents were raised during the Wild West Era, mostly on farms and on the frontier. My maternal grandmother was born in the 1880s, raised in western Montana, and, shortly after she was married, she and my grandfather homesteaded a parcel of land in Alberta, Canada. They lived in a little shack miles from nowhere and Grand Dad was dry land farming. It was a humble existence to say the least. My grandmother went on to live through two World Wars and the Great Depression. She was a tough lady who knew how to get the mostest for the leastest! She squeezed twelve cents out of every dime she ever had. My dad used to joke that she could slice roast beef so thin you could read a newspaper through it. My experience was that he was right; what's more, you only got one slice!

It is difficult in our affluent society to comprehend what people of that era went through just to do the simple every day chores that we hardly give a second thought. When we want to wash some clothes, we just throw a load in the washer, come back in an hour or two, take the clothes out of the washer and throw them in the dryer. Grandma didn't have an automatic washer or electricity and unless she was one of the lucky few, she didn't have water in the house. She had to carry water from the well to the house and heat it on the wood stove. Fire wood was not that easy to come by either when you live in the middle of a prairie! After she got the wash water heated, she washed the clothes by hand on a scrub board, and then had to get rinse water. After she got them on the clothes line to dry, she hoped and prayed there wouldn't be a dust storm.

Granddad's work was not any easier; He had livestock to care for, fences to mend, and all the usual ranch chores that take about 26 hrs a day to get done. He had a tractor, which in the early 1900s was a luxury almost unheard of. But he was dry land farming and had a lot of acres to plow, plant, and harvest. If something broke down, he was looking at a day or two on horse back to get to town and back. When he got to town, they would probably have to order what he needed, so he was better off to stay home and make the part he needed.

This is the environment my mother was born into in 1916. I was born in 1940, the middle ground between the "Greatest Generation" and the "Baby Boomers." I would like to introduce you to a few people from the "Greatest Generation" that helped to form my values.

My father died when I was nine years old. My mother, faced with raising two children, was certainly eligible to receive welfare. She refused to apply for it because she didn't want the "stigma" that came with being a welfare recipient. And there was an attitude about people on welfare. Most people were too polite to say it, but unless you were in a full body cast, they were thinking "Why don't you get a job, ya lazy bum?"

Everyone got knocked down once in while, but they got back up, dusted themselves off, and got back to work. There were plenty of people to offer them a hand to get up. This was acceptable. It was when you got knocked down and didn't try to get up, that you got this "stigma" of being a welfare recipient.

Mom got a helping hand from her brother-in-law. Not a hand-out, but an opportunity to work in his appliance store until she could get on her feet and find a job where she would be able to support herself. She found that job at Wolford's Market. She worked for Harold "Hap" Wolford for seventeen years as a checker. I think Hap Wolford helped Mom more over the years than any one else, but again, not in hand outs. She earned everything she got! And held her head up high while she did it. I think it was Hap that loaned Mom the money to buy her house. It was next to impossible for a single woman to get a mortgage in 1950.

I was only 10 years old and Hap put me to work sweeping floors and stocking shelves. I know now that it was just to keep me occupied and out of trouble after school until Mom got off work. I don't even remember what he paid me; it wasn't much. I am sure it was below minimum wage. Today he would be fined or thrown in jail on some kind of child slavery charge. I came out of it with a foundation of work ethics and a feeling that I was contributing.

I remember Mom sitting my sister and me down and telling us "How it was". She told us that she would be able to feed us, keep a roof over our heads and buy us the bare necessities. Anything else we wanted, we were on our own. We would just have to find a way to earn the money to buy what we wanted. Birthday and Christmas presents were always something like new shoes or a jacket. I earned my spending money from paper routes, one in the morning and one in the afternoon. My sister did babysitting to earn her money.

When I was eleven or twelve years old I got to know Norris Olson. He was one of my paper route customers and lived a couple of blocks from me. I don't think I have ever known a person who was more giving of himself. As a boy growing up without a Dad, I know Norris helped to fill a big empty spot in my life. He was about 30 years old at the time and had a wife and two little toddlers of his own. As busy as he was, he always seemed to have time for me.

He built a little car out of some scrap water pipe and an old Maytag washing machine motor. In spite of my being in his way most of the time, he managed to build it and make me feel like I built it with his help. In the process he taught me the basics of welding and turning a wrench. Every kid in the neighborhood put many a mile on that little car running up and down the streets and sidewalks, grinning from ear to ear while they did. It makes me shudder to think of how many law suits and traffic citations a deed like that could generate today.

The first thing that would have Norris in hot water today was his yard. Norris and his brother Ken were gyppo loggers and there were all kinds of junk lying around: a Caterpillar, equipment trailer, scrap iron, old cable and a couple of broken down cars. You could even find where he had poured some used motor oil to settle the dust. (gasp)

At that time people pretty much made do with what they had and what they could make. They did what ever they had to, to "get err done". Not being able to afford a new pick-up like everyone has today, they took an old Chevy four door sedan, cut the back half of the body off. Built a flat bed on it, hung a canvas over the hole behind the front seat and they had a pick-up!

In today's world there would be some talk around the neighborhood as to why there were so many kids around his house all the time. What's going on when nobody's looking?

While I was in the Navy, Norris left town, and I never saw him again. He went back to school and became a dentist in Beaverton, OR. In 2000 I found his phone number in Beaverton and gave him a call. I am so thankful, that after almost fifty years, I had the opportunity to thank him and tell him how much he meant to me.

My Aunt Mae ranks very high on my list of favorite people. She was like a second mother to me. I spent a lot of time at her house while Mom was working. If nothing else she taught me how to laugh. In the days before TV, family's relied on people like Mae to lighten their work load with laughter. She loved to play practical jokes. She had sort of a sophisticated or pious air about her and beware the unwary; she could sneak up on you! It didn't take you long to learn to check for a "whoopee cushion" before you sat down in her house. She fixed chicken noodle soup for lunch one time. I wasn't even suspicious, until I had a mouth full of rubber bands.

After Sally and I were married and started our family, we bought our first house. Unbeknownst to us we moved in next door to a National Treasure — Herb and Anna Adams. Herb and Anna were about eighty at the time. Herb was one day older than Anna; He said he always felt a man should be older than his wife! They had been married for sixty years and still acted like newlyweds. They did every thing together.

Herb and Anna were not very fashion conscious. Anna always wore a print dress with buttons all the way down the front and always had an apron on. Her hair was always in a bun, either on top or in back. I doubt if she ever had a perm in her life.

Herb always wore slacks, his "everyday slacks" were probably older than I was at the time and had a few patches on them. You could usually tell by looking at his shirt what he had eaten in the last couple of days.

They had very little in material possessions. They didn't have a car; they would walk to town to do their shopping. Herb would put on a necktie and a suit jacket. Sometimes the suit jacket didn't match the slacks and the flower print tie didn't go to well with the checkered shirt. Anna would put on her best apron, and off they would go with their little two wheeled cart in tow.

One of my first projects when we moved in was to build a fence about fifty feet long between our back yard and Herb and

Anna's yard. Our first son was just starting to walk and our second son was due to arrive in a couple of months, and we wanted them fenced in. I bought the materials and almost had them unloaded when Herb and Anna came over. They wanted to pay for half of the fence. I didn't know them very well yet, but it was obvious to me that it would screw up their budget for a couple of months, so I declined their offer. They insisted on helping me build it. I said OK, thinking to myself that they would be in the road more than being helpful.

We went to work and got the posts in the ground and a few of the rails between the posts. Then I got called to go to work. I was driving for Greyhound, working the "extra board". It was the next afternoon, about 24 hours after I left, when I got home. There was Herb and Anna putting the last coat of paint on our new picket fence. And they had put the pickets on my side of the fence!

They had a large front porch with a couch swing. They spent a lot of time sitting and watching the world go by. It was sort of a neighborhood meeting place. Herb had quite a sense of humor. We were sitting on the porch visiting when a lady about 70 years old walked by. She reminded me of my grandmother. Herb said "One nice thing about getting old is, the older you get, the more good looking women there are!"

Not once did I ever hear either one of them say a bad word about anyone or anything. If they didn't have anything good to say, they didn't say anything. Dog-gone-it was about as foul as it got. Every Sunday they went to church. Herb would have a clean white shirt, and his jacket and slacks would match. Anna would wear her best dress. If the weather was bad, usually someone from the church would come by and give them a ride. If not they walked. They always remembered our kids on their birthdays and Christmas. Even if it was nothing more than a card and a hug, you knew it came from the heart.

After living next door to them for about five years we heard a frantic knock on the front door late one evening. It was Herb, He said something was wrong, He couldn't wake up Anna! They had fallen asleep watching TV, and Anna just never woke up. She was gone.

A couple of weeks later I saw Herb sitting in the porch swing. I went over to visit awhile and see how he was doing. He said it was awful lonesome, and he was finding out that he wasn't near as good a cook as Anna was. Then he said, "I thank God every day for taking my Anna before He took me, so that she didn't have to suffer through this loneliness". To this day, forty some years later, when ever I hear the word "Love" a picture of Herb sitting there with tears running down his cheek comes to my mind.

I think of people like Herb and Anna, with how little they had and they wanted for nothing. It wasn't just Herb and Anna; the whole generation was like that. They were content with what they had whether it was a little or a lot. Their happiness was not based on material possessions; it was based on their love of God, country, and family. It wasn't like they weren't trying to better themselves, they were. They had their priorities in order. To them the material stuff was just that. "Stuff"! They make quite a stark comparison with the "now" generation with their new cars, pickups, boat, expensive house, plasma TV, cell phone, I-pods and that "Is this all there is" expression on their face!

The era of rugged individualism has just about died off. We have become an entitlement prone society that wants the government to do just about everything but tuck us in bed at night. Morality and just common courtesy has gone downhill. Most of the negative changes in my life time have happened in the last twenty or thirty years. Strange, but that is the same time span that the majority of The Greatest Generation has gone home to the Lord.

I recently received one of those "funnies" we all get in our e-mail everyday. I think the unknown author nailed one of the major contributing factors in the decline of our morality and the main reason the greatest generation was great. The article was titled, "Different Drug Problem,"

"The other day, someone at a store in our town read that a methamphetamine lab had been found in an old farm house in the adjoining county and he asked me a rhetorical question, "Why didn't we have a drug problem when you and I were growing up?"

I replied I had a drug problem when I was young: I was drug to church on Sunday morning. I was drug to church for weddings and funerals. I was drug to family reunions and community socials no matter the weather.

I was drug by my ears when I was disrespectful to adults. I was also drug to the woodshed when I disobeyed my parents, told a lie, brought home a bad report card, did not speak with respect, spoke ill of the teacher or the preacher, or if I didn't put forth my best effort in everything that was asked of me.

I was drug to the kitchen sink to have my mouth washed out with soap if I uttered a profanity. I was drug out to pull weeds in mom's garden and flower beds and cockleburs out of dad's fields. I was drug to the homes of family, friends and neighbors to help out some poor soul who had no one to mow the yard, repair the clothesline, or chop some firewood, and if my mother had ever known that I took a single dime as a tip for this kindness, she would have drug me back to the woodshed.

Those drugs are still in my veins and they affect my behavior in everything I do say or think. They are stronger than cocaine, crack or heroin; and if today's children had this kind of a drug problem, America would be a better place. God bless the parents who drugged us."

Thank you Mr. Unknown, We needed that!

CHAPTER
TWELVE

WELFARE MENTALITY

I believe that our government has grown into a bloated monster with an insatiable appetite for our tax dollars. We have all experienced the inefficient wasteful ways of our government; there are endless government departments and programs that could be trimmed way back or eliminated altogether. For instance, welfare could be handled much more efficiently on the local level through the churches and friends / relatives. There is a need to provide for members of our society that because of mental or physical disabilities are unable to work and provide for their own needs. I have no doubt that we could give those individuals a much higher standard of living, which they deserve, if we plugged all the holes in the "welfare bucket."

Organizations like St. Vincent De Paul or The Salvation Army are way more efficient than government when it comes to helping the needy. Instead of mailing checks to an endless list of anonymous names, the help is handed out one on one, face to face. The people helping and the people being helped are members of the same community. Relationships are formed and when the needy person starts viewing the help as an entitlement, tough love enters the picture. Somebody can tell them its time to get a job!

Most people agree that it is unwise to enable a drug addict or alcoholic. Why is it wise to enable an able-bodied person who would rather sponge off society than work?

Why is it that few people will give a needy person fifty bucks to help them out, but will vote for a politician that will take that fifty bucks in taxes and give the needy person five?

Jesus said, and as always, time has proved Him right. "The poor will always be with you".

People in need, need a hand-up. Not a hand-out! We should measure welfare's success by how many leave welfare, not by how many are added. Welfare's purpose should be to eliminate its need for existence.

Thomas Jefferson said:

> *"The democracy will cease to exist when you take away from those who are willing to work, and give to those who would not."*

How did George Washington feel about welfare? In a letter to Mr. Peake, the manager of Mt. Vernon, Washington wrote in 1775 while fighting in the Revolutionary War:

> *"Let the hospitality of the house with respect to the poor be kept up. Let no one go hungry away. If any of this kind of people should be in want of corn, supply their necessities, provided it does not encourage them in idleness; and I have no objection to you giving my money in charity to the amount of forty or fifty pounds a year, when you think it is well bestowed. What I mean by having no objection is that it is my desire that it should be done. You are to consider that neither myself nor wife is now in the way to do these kind of offices."*

Mr. Peake, said after the war:

> *"I had orders from General Washington to fill a corn house every year for the sole use of the poor in my neigh-*

borhood, to whom it was a most seasonable and precious relief; saving numbers of poor women and children from extreme want, and blessing them with plenty."

Some would say that I lack compassion for the homeless and needy. Actually, just the opposite is true. I just have a different outlook than our government on how to help them. I like the way it worked in the days before government got involved. Not only is government inefficient and wasteful, it denies the giver the grace that they would receive by loving their neighbor. There is a power that is lost in government welfare, the power of relationships and respect of one another that bond us together as a people.

Put them on welfare and in low cost government housing, then they are penalized when they earn any money by a decrease in benefits. It is a system that encourages people to lie and it destroys what little spark of initiative they have and drives a wedge of division between the haves and have-nots. Then we end up with another career welfare recipient. I think that is the main objective for government in this 'rob Peter to pay Paul' program. Government wants as many Paul's as they can get; they can always count on Paul's vote.

We seem to have a warped sense of what poverty is. We have the richest poor people on earth. The poor in our society today have way more than my family had when I was growing up, and I did not feel like I was poor. I could look around at other kids and see a lot of them that had less than I had. The poor today seem to have as much as the middle class did in the 1950s, and our government wants us to feel guilty about it!

There was a poll on MSN recently on what was considered necessities, I don't remember how many items were on the list, but there were things like automobile, T.V., computer, clothes dryer, microwave, cell phone, cable or satellite hook up. I had to chuckle when I realized that the only item on the list that was in my home while I was growing up was a T.V. And I was about thirteen when we got that. When I was a kid the necessities were food, clothing and shelter.

My wife Sally and I have some first hand experience with helping the homeless. For ten years we were the directors of the "Hot Meal" program at our church. We have countless heart-warming memories from that experience. There were many who had been knocked down and were trying to get on their feet again. One of the first lessons we learned was that you cannot help people unless they want to help themselves. There were also the ones addicted to drugs or alcohol who joined us for a meal and were just working the system for whatever they could get for nothing. We welcomed them knowing that people on drugs or alcohol will sooner or later hit bottom from where there is nowhere to go but up. With the relationships we had built with them, when they did hit bottom we were the ones they turned to. There was several times that we brought people into our home that had hit bottom and let them live with us until they got on their feet. Some made it and went on with life, others got knocked down again.

We had one lady from Mexico that needed help. She would bring her four little girls in to feed them. Her husband deserted her and the children. She had a job washing dishes at a local restaurant. One day she came in and thanked us for all our help, then told us she would no longer be coming in to eat, that she had a new job with a pay raise and that she was able to make it on her own now. She did continue to come in when she was able and help in the kitchen.

I remember reading about a group of Revolutionary War volunteers reporting to their unit to fight in the war. Upon arrival they were offered a meal. They declined and broke out the beans and hardtack they had brought with them. They did not feel their government should feed them! How far we have come!

CHAPTER
THIRTEEN

TAXES, TAXES AND MORE TAXES

If all of the taxes that each of us pays every year were collected in the form of one bill, due April 15th each year, we would have a modern day Boston Tea Party on our hands. Our legislators in Washington have been using devious means to collect taxes for so long that their methods aren't even thought of as devious. Have you ever noticed that Election Day is in November and tax day is in April, just about as far apart as possible? I think we should have Election Day on April 16th.

Intercepting your tax dollars with payroll withholding before you receive them has a numbing effect on the pain of paying taxes. Most people would feel the pain if they actually had the cash in hand and had to write a check to the government, especially if you had to include the half of Social Security the employer pays. If you think that isn't coming out of your pocket, think again. That is part of what it cost the employer to have you work for him. If you were not working for him he wouldn't be paying it.

Our legislators never want to come right out in the open and say they are going to raise taxes; they always go around to the back door and raise fees, add fifty cents to a pack of cigarettes or a bottle of booze. Then there is always their favorite, raising corporate taxes. Most voters don't realize that corporate taxes are coming directly out of their pocket. We just elected a new president who ran on the line of "cutting taxes for the middle class." "Tax those greedy corporations." Most people said, "Sounds great! I think I'll vote for him." What is really going on here?

You go in a store and buy a widget. That store is one of those greedy corporations. The widget you bought was delivered to the store by a trucking company, which is another greedy corporation. The trucking company picked up the widget from a wholesale warehouse that is another greedy corporation. There was another greedy corporate trucking company that delivered the widget to the wholesale warehouse from the manufacturer that is another greedy corporation. The manufacturer bought raw materials from more greedy corporations that were delivered by truck or rail. I could go on and on with this, but I think you can see the point. There are a lot of corporate entities behind anything you buy. Now, "The dirty little secret." **Corporations do not pay taxes!**

The short course of business 101: Your income must exceed your outgo or you won't be in business long! It doesn't matter if it's the world's largest corporation or your paper boy, the same rule applies. You have income on one side of the ledger and expenses on the other side. Subtract expenses from the income, and that is your profit. Taxes go on the expense side; they are another cost of doing business just like labor, light bill, cost of the building, etc. etc. The cost of doing business determines the price of the product or service. In other words, when you bought your widget you helped pay the taxes of each and every corporation involved. Have you bought a widget lately? It doesn't end there either. All of those corporations buy products to conduct their business, from trucks to computers to paper clips.

When they buy those products, they are in the same boat you were when buying the widget. They helped pay the taxes for all the corporations involved in their purchase, which adds to their cost of doing business. It has a snow ball effect. And don't forget you just paid 7% or 8% sales tax on all those hidden taxes you paid!

What it all boils down to is we don't have a clue what we are paying in taxes! I think if we did, the revolt would begin. Ultimately it is the consumer, you and I, the buying public that pay all corporate taxes. It is time for us as the tax payers to regain control of the purse stings. If you are a parent and have forty year old kids still living at home sponging off Mom and Dad, there comes a time when you have to kick them out and tell them to get a job!

CHAPTER
FOURTEEN

WHERE DO WE GO FROM HERE?

There is no doubt that our nation is in dire straits, and if corrective measures are not taken now we will no longer be a free nation! So what needs to be done? How do we fix it? I certainly do not have all the answers; one thing I do know for sure is that Ronald Reagan was right. Government is not the solution, government is the problem!

The secular anti-God movement has been at work since the very birth of our nation, for the first 140 years they had to use stealth and clandestine methods to gain toe holds and traction for their agenda. It wasn't until the 1930s and the FDR administration that their efforts started to gain momentum, and they were able to weave their poisonous agenda and policies into the bureaucracy of our government. It was still several more decades of sneaking around in the shadows and behind closed doors before the veil started to lift enough that we saw glimpses of the face of evil. And evil is exactly what it is! The progressives are throwing God under the bus and replacing Him with the rule of man. Any way you want to cut it, that is evil!

To restore our nation to the founding principles we have a long hard row to hoe! It is not something that will be fixed in a year or two, but we have to stop the momentum of the progressive agenda and get it going the other direction **now**. One advantage we have is that the absolute moral truth of God is on our side. It can stand in the light of day and we will not have to sneak around in the shadows to gain traction for our message like the progressives had to do. People want to hear the truth; they have wallowed around in the gray fog of relativism long enough.

There is a revolt on the horizon right now; the progressives have disturbed the sleeping giant and he is waking up. I hope it will be a bloodless revolution in which the battles can be fought in the ballot box, but don't count on it. The progressives will not relinquish the gains they have made in the last 200 years without a fight.

We have to pull back the drapes and let the sun shine on the evil in our country and educate the American people on the methods and techniques of the progressives. We must know the enemy so that we recognize him when we see him because they are all around us and coming into our living rooms every day on the TV, radio and newspapers.

They are in our schools and universities; they are in the halls of justice and in our county, state and federal governments.

Everyone should be familiar with Saul Alinsky and his teachings. Saul Alinsky (1909-1972) was a Marxist grassroots organizer who formulated tactical battle plans for the radical left. He wrote *"Reveille for Radicals"* (1946) and *"Rules for Radicals"* (1971) which outlined his organizational principles and strategies. His teachings were put into practice by the anti-establishment '60s radicals and revolutionaries. Alinsky taught "true revolutionaries do not flaunt their radicalism; they cut their hair, put on suits, and infiltrate the system from within". They moved slowly and patiently to penetrate universities, political parties, churches, and labor unions. The old Democratic Party of fifty years ago has been taken over by the successful use of Alinsky tactics. Alinsky recruited a young student named Hillary Rodham. He considered

Hillary a terrific organizer and wanted her to become his protégé, but she had her sights set higher! She learned her lessons well. The Clintons excelled at using Alinsky tactics.

Barack Obama mastered the Alinsky methods so well he ended up teaching workshops on them! He worked four years as a community organizer with an Alinsky group called the Developing Communities Project. When you become familiar with the Alinsky methods they are easy to spot, and there is a lot of them in the Obama administration and the Democratic Party. I can't help but to recall the statement made by Nikita Khrushchev in 1960, "We will defeat you without firing a shot; we will do it from within".

We need to look at history for direction and follow principles that are time tested and proven to work. The Holy Bible is a lot of different things to a lot of different people. One thing it is, for sure, it is a history of mankind. There is a theme that occurs over and over and over through out scripture. It is when God's people are in God's favor and place their trust in Him, they win their battles, when not—they lose.

I hope the message is simple enough that we can all grasp it without having to line up collectively as a nation and stick our finger in the light socket.

We must, as individuals, as families, towns, states, and as a nation turn to God and ask for His forgiveness and His guidance. We must ask him to bring forth leaders who are Christian statesmen who will lead us through this battle. Without this step, there is not a doubt in my mind—this ship is sinking.

We must come together as one people with one purpose. One nation, under God, indivisible, with liberty and justice for all. The time has come for all Americans to ask themselves some hard questions. Do we trust in God or do we trust in government? Is God in control, or is government in control? Are we one nation, under God, indivisible, with liberty and justice for all? Or would you rather have one nation under government, divisible, with whatever liberty and justice the government wants to dole out to us? We can't have it both ways. And with no action it will be the latter.

A quote from Ezra Stiles (1727-1795) (Minister / Lawyer / Yale College President):

> *"As all the tops of corn in a waving field are inclined in one direction by a gust of wind, in like manner the Governor of the world has given one and the same universal bent of inclination to the whole body of our people."*

> *"Is it the work of man that thirteen States, frequently quarrelling about boundaries, clashing in interests, differing in politics, manners, customs, forms of government, and religion, scattered over an extensive continent, under the influence of a variety of local prejudices, jealousies, and aversions, should all harmoniously agree as if one mighty mind inspired the whole?"*

As the old adage goes, we must pray like it all depends on God and work like it all depends on us. Between now and the 2010 election we must do whatever we can to prevent further damage and to wake up the people who are still oblivious of what is taking place. Talk to your neighbors, write letters to the editor, and call your senators and representatives. Do whatever you can; I decided to write a book. I know that when you have senators like I do, Barbara Boxer and Dianne Feinstein, it seems like a waste of time. I might as well call "Loony Tunes" and talk to Daffy Duck. They just blow a little smoke at you in a form letter telling you all the great things they are doing to destroy our country and keep on trucking. But do it anyway. We have to do more than put a bumper snicker on the car.

In the 2010 election we need to clean house in Congress and the Senate. Anyone who voted for the stimulus bill without reading it should be sent packing. If they are secular anti-God and vote for anti-God bills, they should be sent packing.

Even if they are the best senator or congressman you have ever seen if they have finished their second term they should be sent home. In Congress, seniority equals corruption. If in doubt, kick them out! The Founding Fathers never intended that we have "career politicians" in the first place. Ever wonder why someone would spend millions every four years for a job that pays $170,000 a year. I doubt if it's the dental plan.

George Washington never collected his salary while he was General of the Army in the Revolutionary War, nor as President of the United States for eight years. He was a soldier and a statesman who served his country for no gain and tremendous sacrifice. I am not saying our leaders should work for no salary; I am just pointing out the contrast between George Washington and the self-serving crooks we have now. We need to define the line between serving your country and ripping off your country!

The 2010 election will be just the beginning; we have to prepare for the 2012 election and clean house again with the congressmen who were not up for re-election in 2010. We have a long "must do" list and I don't know what the sequence is. That could become a discussion similar to which is the most important leg on the kitchen table.

We need to reinstate the checks and balances, get all of the secular activist judges off of the federal courts, and restore the courts to their original function of interpreting law and holding the executive and legislative branches within their constitutional boundaries. The states need to follow the lead of Oklahoma, Texas, Montana, and Utah which are the first of the states to reclaim their sovereignty and to declare that they are not under the federal government directives. (Bet you didn't hear that on the evening news).

We need to enforce the Tenth Amendment and de-centralize the government. There are endless examples where the federal government has overstepped the constitutional boundaries and trampled on the states sovereignty. Every function of government that can be carried out on the state level should be and the federal agency abolished. A good example would be the U.S. Forest Service. Every state can manage the forest within its boundaries.

Why do we need National Forests? Why should the federal government own any land other than Washington D.C.? The benefits of eliminating the forest service would be numerous. Besides eliminating a bloated, wasteful bureaucracy, states that are having less than desirable results in managing their forest can emulate the successful states. With a controversial issue like school vouchers, if states wanted to experiment with it, they could and the other states could see benefits and liabilities without putting the whole national school system in jeopardy. The same would hold true with all the other agencies, like national parks, education, bureau of land management, etc. The list of federal agencies could pass for a phone book.

One advantage to the power being with the states instead of the federal government is the taxes now going to the federal government would either be staying in the taxpayers pocket or going to the states. Competition is good in the business world to keep prices lower for the consumer. It would work the same way with taxes among the states. If taxes were too high in one state, people and industry could move to another state with lower taxes. You can't do that now when the federal tax is too high.

And speaking of taxes, we need to abolish the progressive income tax, all corporate taxes, capital gains tax, estate tax and go to a fairer tax, preferably a national sales tax.   Have everything right up front, in one tax, where we can see what we are paying. Instead of a tax code that you would have trouble cramming into the trunk of your car, it could be reduced to a couple of sentences. Instead of having almost ninety thousand IRS employees, we could probably have less than a thousand. The rest could go get a job in the private sector and help pull the wagon instead of riding in it.

With a sales tax we would bring the underground economy above ground, prostitutes, gamblers, drug dealers, and the like would pay their taxes just like the rest of us. I have seen estimates that there is as much as ten trillion dollars in overseas accounts hiding from the IRS. Seems to me that it would make more sense to remove the incentive to hide money overseas, bring that money home, and turn it loose in our economy instead of spending $800 billion borrowed and/or printed dollars like our servants in Washington just did with the stimulus bill.

A sales tax would eliminate what James Madison described as the opportunity and temptation of a predominant party to trample on the rules of justice. The tax code could no longer be used to reward friends and punish opponents, and it could not be used for social engineering. Everyone should be paying the same rate and everyone will have an equal interest in keeping the tax low. To have a large bloc of voters impose a tax on a smaller bloc of voters is not the American way, even if we have been doing it for close to a hundred years. There will still be those who say the rich should pay more, the rich will pay more. A person who spends a million dollars a year will pay 50 times the tax a person who spends 20 thousand a year will pay.

We need term limits! Term limits are the only way we can keep our representatives in touch with the real world. Instead of slick talking lawyers turned career politician, I would rather see people with calluses on their hands who have drawn out their retirement money and mortgaged their home to start a business, who know the feeling of bankruptcy nipping at their backside when everything they own is on the line. It would be refreshing to get a "yep" or "nope" in response to a direct question instead of a ten minute condescending philosophical diatribe (big words for a truck driver) that still leaves you wondering whether that was a yes or a no.

Every profession has its "tricks of the trade," but in the halls of Congress there is no room for tricks of the trade. The tricks are always pulled on the taxpayer and the representative's purpose is to represent the taxpayer. Every bill should be a stand alone bill; if it can't stand on its own merit, it shouldn't be there. The practice of ear marks and slipping a controversial bill through on the coattails of a "must pass bill" is deception and just plain dishonest.

Gerrymandering is another dishonest practice that must be stopped. I cannot believe how such a blatant corruption of our election process was ever allowed in the first place, let alone become a common practice. Instead of the voters selecting their representative, the representative is selecting the voter. There are very simple solutions, and the fact that this practice has not been curtailed shows the representative's interest leans more toward re-election than the good of the nation. All it would take is a law stating that every Congressional district must consist of four straight lines, two north-south and two east-west, forming a rectangular shape approximately the same height and width and the only exception being with the boundaries which fall on a state border.

There needs to be something done about the lobbyist in Washington. There is something like 37,000 lobbyists, with 535 senators and representatives, that is about 70 lobbyists per representative pushing for legislation on special interest projects. Way too many of them represent foreign governments that do not have the best interest of the United States at heart. What really turns my stomach is the number of former congressmen, top government employees, and even past presidents making millions lobbying for foreign governments. The insiders are highly prized as lobbyist; they know which strings to pull and what buttons to push to obtain results like the recent Pentagon defense contract for Air Force refueling air tankers going to Airbus instead of Boeing. Airbus is a French company that is ultimately owned by Dubai. So we end up with a foreign country building our military aircraft and 44,000 fewer jobs at Boeing, in addition to the $40 billion of our tax dollars going to a foreign nation. To me this is a little more than bordering on treason. Personally, I wish tarring and feathering was still politically correct!

Our elected officials will never make these changes without a fight; they do not want to relinquish the power to the people.

History has shown that liberty lost is very seldom regained. We the people will have to demand that the changes be made through the ballot box, by electing Christian statesmen who know what mere politicians never perceive—that the character, not the bank account, is the real backbone of a nation.

If we want our children and grandchildren to live in a free country, we better get our heads out of the sand and get busy!

Author Biography

After my father died when I was nine years old, I learned at a young age there is no free lunch. If I wanted something I would have to earn it. I have always been an independent person, always taking the road less traveled. I was not a good student in school. My mother forced me to finish high school with threats of bodily harm. It's not that I was stupid, lazy, or didn't want to learn. I just wanted to learn what I wanted to learn and not the stuff they were trying to teach me. While I was flunking high school English, I was reading things like Winston Churchill's *The Gathering Storm* and Edward Gibbons' *The Decline and Fall of The Roman Empire.*

I joined the Navy right out of high school and was a nuclear weapons technician on the aircraft carrier *U.S.S. Coral Sea* and was discharged in 1962. At that point in my life, if it didn't have wheels, boobs, or come in a little brown bottle, it couldn't hold my interest for long. After realizing there is no demand for an A-bomb mechanic in civilian life and not finding a way I could legally and morally support myself drinking beer and chasing girls, I started driving for a living. I am sure I could have found a more lucrative line of work, but money has never been what motivated me. In 1972 my wife and I quit our jobs, sold our house, and moved our three small boys to the Bohemia Mountains in Oregon to live on a gold mine. I did better than most gold miners; it took me four years to go broke. Financially speaking, that was undoubtedly the dumbest thing I have ever done. As a life experience for our young family, living the pioneer life style for four years was priceless! My mother-in-law told me years ago, "You're a pioneer without a frontier." I think she had me pegged!

Synopsis

"The Assault on Liberty" is the common sense opinion of a professional truck driver on the need to return to the basic principals upon which our Founding Fathers built this nation. By throwing God under the bus, we are also throwing our liberty and freedom under the bus.